Healing Heroes: Rose Quartz

To Susan...
Always shine your light!
Mari

Written by **Manijeh Hart**   Illustrated by **Xander A. Nesbitt**

Affirm:

"I am connected to nature.

I am the light of the sun.

I am always growing.

Change is good."

This book is dedicated to all the children big and small who want to remember the light they have inside.

Healing Heroes are a group of superheroes with the power and energy of the crystals and gemstones of Mother Earth.

.

Healing Heroes come to the rescue when children are feeling unhappy, upset, scared, worried, stuck, rejected, lonely, unfocused, angry, or in need of a confidence boost. Healing Heroes reassure children by equipping them with crystals or gemstones and affirmations to match. Each book in the series highlights a Healing Hero and provides daily affirmations for children to repeat as they face their problem.

.

Before children know it, their spirits will be lifted and full of self—love and comfort. Healing Heroes always show up when they are needed. With Healing Heroes, children have personal superhero friends to remind them of their own light and inner peace.

Meet Rose Quartz

Self-love

Love with others

Peace

Harmony

Balance

JUST-IN: Akeem tried out for the basketball team. The team roster was announced and he didn't hear his name. He feels disappointed in himself.

TO THE RESCUE: Rose Quartz

"I accept myself.

I love who I am.

I love who I will be.

 I love me."

JUST-IN: Maria knew the answer to the question. She raised her hand and even started waving it a little. Her teacher still called on another student. Maria felt invisible.

"My heart is full of joy

 I love who I am.

I feel love every day

My heart is happy."

JUST-IN: Jason's parents work a lot and they are always too tired to do anything fun when they are home. Jason wonders if they care about him.

TO THE RESCUE: Rose Quartz

"I love myself.

Love shines in me.

Love shines around me.

I am special."

JUST-IN: Bria feels jealous of her little sister. She's always getting attention. Everyone tells her how cute she is and wants to take her picture. Bria thinks everyone forgot about her.

"I am free to love me.

I love myself first.

I am a special person.

My heart shines bright."

JUST–IN: Priya wished her mom could see how much her words hurt her. She didn't do things on purpose to annoy her. Priya just wanted attention and love. Her mom made her feel worthless.

"I am love.

I believe in myself.

I only accept good things.

I trust my inner voice."

Reflection & Connection

Name a person or thing that you love. Why?

What do you love about yourself?

Why is it important to love yourself?

How do you show love to others?

Create your own affirmation for when you want to feel more LOVE!

I am _____.

I am _____.

I am _____.

About the Author

As a former elementary school teacher, Manijeh Hart has witnessed the impact of social-emotional support during a child's formative years. She believes that when a child feels loved, safe, and valued, there is no limit to their potential. Manijeh included yoga, meditation, and daily affirmations with children to support them when they felt upset, angry, or unsure. Through these mindfulness strategies, children became more confident and aware of their ability to bring themselves peace.

Message from the Author: Being in the classroom for 14 years afforded me the special opportunity to share space with children who came to school with very real problems that affected their self-esteem, identity, and outlook on life. I created Healing Heroes to share words of affirmation with children in classrooms and communities across the world. With this series, I hope to support children in connecting with their inner light and unique essence.

26862794R00015